WITHDRAWN

SOLIDS • LIQUIDS • GASES

A Buddy Book

by

Julie Murray

ABDO
Publishing Company

VISIT US AT
www.abdopublishing.com

Published by ABDO Publishing Company, 4940 Viking Drive, Edina, Minnesota 55435.

Copyright © 2007 by Abdo Consulting Group, Inc. International copyrights reserved in all countries. No part of this book may be reproduced in any form without written permission from the publisher. Buddy Books™ is a trademark and logo of ABDO Publishing Company.

Printed in the United States.

Series Coordinator: Sarah Tieck
Contributing Editor: Michael P. Goecke
Graphic Design: Maria Hosley
Cover Photograph: Photos.com
Interior Photographs/Illustrations: Media Bakery, Photos.com

Library of Congress Cataloging-in-Publication Data

Murray, Julie, 1969–
    Solids, liquids, and gases / Julie Murray.
       p. cm. — (First science)
    Includes index.
    ISBN-13: 978-1-59679-830-4
    ISBN-10: 1-59679-830-0
    1. Matter—Properties—Juvenile literature. I. Title. II. Series: Murray, Julie, 1969- First science.

QC173.36.M87 2006
530.4—dc22
                                                              2006017159

TABLE OF CONTENTS

THE FACTS ABOUT FORMS

Solids, liquids, and gases are a big part of everyday life. These are the three forms of **matter**. They are also an important feature of the natural world.

Look around. The roads people drive on are a solid. The air they breathe is a gas. The water people drink is a liquid.

It is easy to see solids, liquids, and gases in action in many places.

Bikers ride on solid surfaces, such as roads. People breathe in oxygen, which is a gas.

People drink liquids, such as water.

THE SCIENCE OF SOLIDS, LIQUIDS, AND GASES

The key to the science of liquids, solids, and gases is **matter**.

Everything on Earth is matter. Anything that takes up space is matter. Matter can exist in different forms.

There are three main states of matter. These are liquid, solid, and gas.

Matter can change between the
three different forms.

WHAT MAKES MATTER?

All **matter** is made up of atoms. Atoms are very small. People need to use **microscopes** to see atoms.

Different kinds of atoms can join together. This is called linking. When atoms link, they form bonds and change. Linked atoms are called molecules.

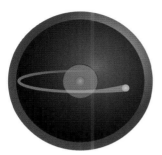

Hydrogen Atom

Oxygen Atom

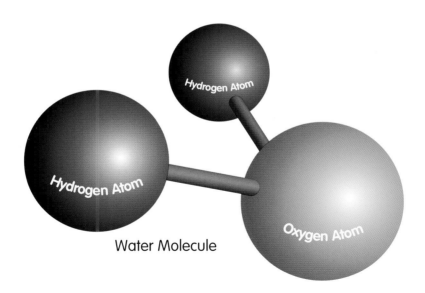

Water Molecule

Hydrogen and oxygen atoms link to make water.

HOW LIQUIDS WORK

Water is an example of **matter** in a liquid form. In liquids, molecules are able to move easily around each other.

Because liquids move freely, they change to match the shape of their container. For example, water takes the shape of whatever cup you drink it from. But, the water takes up the same amount of space in each container.

Orange juice is another example of matter in a liquid state.

.∎ HOW SOLIDS WORK ∎.

When water freezes, it becomes a solid.
Ice is water in a solid form.

Ice cubes are frozen water. When
they melt they become liquid again.

Other examples of solids include rocks and books.

In solids, molecules are close together. This means the molecules aren't able to easily move around each other. So unlike liquids, solids have a shape of their own.

.■ HOW GASES WORK ■.

When water is heated to boiling, it makes steam. Steam is the gas form of water.

Steam rises from the water boiling in this pot.

Helium is a gas that helps balloons float. But, it cannot be seen!

Gases move freely, like liquids. However, they can also **expand** to fill a space. And, they can even **shrink** to fit into a smaller space. Many times, people can't see gases, such as the air.

Glass is another example of something that can exist in more than one form. It can be a liquid or a solid.

When glass is very, very hot, it exists in liquid form. This is how glass can be shaped into different objects. People can do this by hand or by using machines.

When the glass is cooled, it becomes a solid again.

Glassblowers make solid objects from liquid glass.

Many everyday objects are made from glass.

FLOWING, SLIDING, AND FLOATING THROUGH HISTORY

Through the years, many scientists have tried to understand the science of solids, liquids, and gases.

In the 1600s, scientists discovered that **matter** could become gas. Jan Baptista van Helmont was a chemist from Belgium. He was the first person to write about gas.

People use gas in grills and stoves for cooking.

Since these experiments long ago, many people have studied the science of solids, liquids, and gases. And, they have made many important discoveries. Still, most agree there is still more to learn about this science.

SOLIDS, LIQUIDS, AND GASES IN THE WORLD TODAY

Solids, liquids, and gases are a big part of daily life. Without solids, liquids, and gases, people wouldn't exist. Without **matter**, the Earth wouldn't have air or oceans.

Without solids, grass and trees wouldn't exist.
Without liquids, people couldn't fish on lakes.
Without gases, people wouldn't be able to breathe.

The world would be a very different place without solids, liquids, and gases.

Solid rocks hold in the liquid water of a river. Because of this, people can kayak.

.. IMPORTANT WORDS ..

chemistry the study of chemicals.

expand to get bigger.

matter what things are made of.

microscope a tool that scientists use to look closely at very small objects. Some of these objects are too small for the eye to see by itself.

shrink to get smaller.

.. WEB SITES ..

To learn more about **Solids, Liquids, and Gases**, visit ABDO Publishing Company on the World Wide Web. Web site links about **Solids, Liquids, and Gases** are featured on our Book Links page. These links are routinely monitored and updated to provide the most current information available.

www.abdopublishing.com

.. INDEX ..